GREAT THINGS TO BE

KENIN O'CONNOR

 Be Kind.

Be nice, take turns and share.

Show others that you care.

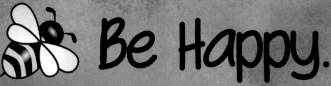 Be Happy.

Be happy every day.
Smile, laugh, have
fun and play.

 Be Thankful.

Count your blessings each morning,
it will start your day off right.
Remember what you are grateful
for when you go to bed at night.

 Be Positive.

Keep a positive attitude, be your own #1 fan. You can do anything if you just believe that you can.

 Be Yourself.

You are special just the way that you are. You are one of a kind, a bright shining star.

🐝 Be Confident.

Believe in yourself and in what you can do. Anything is possible, dreams can come true.

 Be Polite.

Please and thank you are
great things to say. Show good
manners each and every day.

 Be Responsible.

You are in charge of everything you say and do. Think before you act and make the right choice for you.

 Be Friendly.

Everyone is different and special in their own way. Be nice to others and try to make someone's day.

🐝 Be Brave.

Speak up for yourself and always stand your ground. Never let others bully you around.

 Be Honest.

Lies are hurtful to others and to you.
Telling the truth is the right thing to do.

Be Healthy.

It is important to exercise and eat healthy food. It will help you feel great and keep you in a happy mood.

All of the things listed are important you see. Do your best with each one because they are **great things to be.**

Discussion Questions

Parents & Teachers — For interactive fun, use the seek and find feature presented in this book. Ask your little ones to spot the bee hidden in each picture!

Be Kind

What does it mean to be kind?

How is kindness shown in this picture?

What are things that you can do to show kindness to others each day?

When you do something kind for someone, how does that make you feel?

When someone is nice to you, how does that make you feel?

How do you feel when someone is not nice to you?

Be Happy

What does it mean to be happy?

When you think happy thoughts, how does it make you feel? When you think negative or sad thoughts, how does it make you feel? Which way would you rather feel?

Ask the child/children to SMILE. How does that make you feel?

What are things that make you happy?

When you are not feeling happy, what are things that you can do to turn your mood around?

Be Thankful

What does it mean to be thankful?

What is the boy thankful for in this picture?

What are you thankful for?

When you think or talk about the things that you are thankful for, how does that make you feel? When you think or talk about the things you don't have, how does that make you feel? Which way would you rather feel?

Be Positive

What does it mean to be positive?

When you tell yourself that you can do something, how does it make you feel?

What do you think the boy climbing the rock wall was thinking or saying to himself?

When you say things like "I can't do it or I am not good enough," how does that make you feel? Instead of saying those things, what could you say?

What are some positive things that you can say to yourself each day?

Be Yourself

What does it mean to be yourself?

Does the girl in the picture look like the other girls? What is different?

Is it okay to be different?

Does the girl look happy to be herself?

If the other girls in the picture were making fun of her for being different, how do you think that would make her feel?

What are some things that make you special and unique?

Be Confident

What does it mean to be confident?

When you are confident, how does it make you feel?

What are the children in the picture dreaming about becoming when they grow up?

What do you want to become when you grow up?

Be Polite

What does it mean to be polite?

What is happening in this picture? What did the little girl say? Was it polite?

Are there any other things you can say that are polite?

Why is it important to have good manners?

Be Responsible

What does it mean to be responsible?

What do you think the children are saying to the boy that is not going through the fence?

Has anyone ever asked you to do something that you knew that you shouldn't? What did you do? How did you feel?

What do you think the boy in the green shirt is saying?

Be Friendly

What does it mean to be friendly?

Tell the child/children that the boy in the glasses is new to school. He is unsure about where to sit. What do you think the girl is saying to him?

How do you think the boy feels?

Do you think he was nervous about meeting new friends on the first day of school?

Have you ever been nervous about a new situation? How did you feel? Did anyone make you feel more comfortable?

How could you make a new student feel welcome?

Be Brave

What does it mean to be brave?

Do the boys look like they are saying nice things to the boy in the orange shirt?

Why not? How do you think the boy in the orange shirt felt when they were saying not kind things? What do you think he did about it? Did he cry? Did he yell back?

What can you do if someone says unkind words to you?

What are things you can do if you or someone else is being picked on?

<u>Be Honest</u>

What does it mean to be honest?

Is the little boy telling the truth? How do you know?

How does the little sister feel? How do you know?

Sometimes when we do the wrong thing we are afraid to tell the truth. Have you ever felt uncomfortable after you have told a lie?

What could the little boy have said instead of telling a lie?

Be Healthy

What does it mean to be healthy?

What is the boy in the picture eating? What kind of healthy foods do you enjoy eating?

What type of activities are the children in this picture doing?

What type of things do you like to do for exercise?

Why is it important to take care of our bodies?

Made in the USA
Lexington, KY
17 November 2019